Copyright © 2008 by Chazarrae Freeman

Published by Chazarrae Freeman "Free Publishing"

All rights reserved. Printed in the United States of America. No part of this book may be reproduced in any manner whatsoever without the prior written permission of both the copyright owner and the above publisher of this book. For information, Chazarrae Freeman 2087 Olden Avenue, Hamilton, NJ 08610

ISBN-13: 978-0-6152-0491-8

From the Dredges of the Soul

By Chazarrae S. Freeman

Free Publishing 2008

To my beautiful mother who helped affirm the completed good work.

To my father, whose diligence and hardwork will always stand a model.

To God, whose love "dredged" me from the clutches of death.

"When the moment hatches in time's womb there will be no art talk. The only poem you will hear will be the spearpoint pivoted in the punctured marrow of the villain…Therefore we are the last poets of the world"--**South African poet Keorapetse "Willie" Kgositsile**

Special Thanks to Outkast, Dr.Cornel West, Amiri Baraka, Cee-lo Green"The Soul Machine", Toni Morrison, Jill Scott,The Youngstown, Boardman, Sandusky, and New York police departments for their blatant and corrupt abuse of power and the rest of the poetic free thinking community.

Table of Contents
Foreword-pg.6

New and Improved Ways of Saying
"No Blacks allowed"-pg.7
Deception-pg.9
What is Fear?-pg.10
Immortal-pg.12
Black Thought-pg.13
Test-pg.15
Mirrors-pg.17
Trophies-pg.18
Boy meets Girl-pg.19
The Calling-pg.19
Ribs-pg.20
Soulutions-pg.21
W.M.D.-pg.22
El Voz-pg.23
Nine months of Labor-pg.24
Alcoholics Anonymous-pg.26
Types of Stereos-pg.27
Pardon Me-pg.29
Souletry-pg.30
The Love Letter-pg.31
History began with America-pg.33
A Brief Review-pg.36
The Headless Horseman-pg.39
N.I.G.G.A.S. from Another Planet-pg.41
Sound of Music-pg.44
Two Women in the Street Crying-pg.45
Cycle-pg.47
Big Brother-pg.47
Family Tree-pg.48
Just a Thought-pg.49

Grow Up-pg.50
A Note-pg.51
To You-pg.52
A Strange Niceness-pg.53
The Breath-pg.54
A Day in the life of Steve Green-pg.55
Ode to Patriarch-pg.56
To the Eastside-pg.57
My Stubborn Mother-pg.58
Grass-59
Tribute to M.L.K. Jr.-pg. 60
What is Black-pg.61

About the Author-pg.63

Foreword

When I first began writing what is now known as "From the Dredges..." I never knew the inner thoughts I was compelled to record would come to fruition in the form of a book. I would like to believe that it wasn't due to selfishness, but a calling and intuition to wait for maturity in skill and also understanding of my experiences. As you journey through this piece, the maturity itself is evident. When I reflected on the first few works I had written, I was disgusted with their quality. It took every ounce of me to keep from destroying it and etching it out. My skill had to develop from humble beginnings. It would be similar to a denial of the institution of slavery. I believe almost indubitably that history would indeed repeat itself and we would not learn from ourselves. Hence, we learn from our point of origin and the things we have evolved from. That is the significance of this piece: history and heritage. I taught myself to appreciate the growth from the seed. This work developed in unforeseen dimensions. In this book I am truly exposed. It was whom I consulted when I felt no one would understand. It consoled me and allowed me to understand things as they were and to work to change and challenge the status quo through my work. Here is what I learned...

New and Improved ways of saying "*No Blacks Allowed*"

No entry.
No way.
No blacks today.
No rags, No hats,
No braids, No tats'
No shoes, No shirt,
No pride, No work.
No God, No quilts,
No swords with hilts.
No hips, No lips.
Go home red bone.
No gangs of black, only gangs in blue.
I saw—a state of Martial Law.
No singin', No dancin'
No leavin', I mean, No stayin',
No prayin', No learnin'
No, leave them crosses burnin'.
Stopped for No reason,
No rappin', No pleasin'
No school, play ball.
No enroll in the fall.
No women, No land
I know you don't understand.
No abstinence,
Mo' pestilence.
Oh—no dialect, speak English.
Oh yeah, I really mean this.
No money, No problem,
Get the guns and rob 'em.
No president, No rent.
No time to repent.
No hugs, more drugs.

I'm sure they have a cure for…
No AIDS—endure.
No more being whores
Doing free labor and more chores.
No pagers, No cells.
No way out of hell.
Suspended, expelled from
"They schools" to "they jails".
No i.d., No club.
Have i.d.? So what.
No key to the handcuffs,
Opiate for the pain
Take a puff.
I wish there was…
No hate.
No "No's".
Let us procreate.
No predestined life sentences.
No poorly funded schools aiding these
Incidences.
No integration, No relation.
It'll end soon just be patient.
No Asata in the U.S.
No Tupac either, who will lead the rest?
Notorious people for **No**torious things.
Lift every voice 'cause No freedom rings,
Especially with No blacks on the scene.
No hearts, No minds,
And especially, No definitely,
None of your kind.

Deception

Deception is best hidden
Behind the purest face,
Soft in tone,
Assuring you your trust is not misplaced.
It claims to be unknowing,
Pure in all intents,
But inside evil is all that circumvents.
Behind every smile,
Know that the wheels turn
And for her own desires
You will quickly learn:
Little angels can be little imps.
The purest fairies
Can become devilish nymphs.
Two faces one body,
Hideous creatures
Hidden by the lurid smoke of their lair,
In the deepest caverns
With the reddest glare.
Mouse traps, bear traps,
Watch out for her snare
Or you will find out well
The cost for her claim to innocence
When its truly been lost.
For some it may be a few pence,
For others their life,
Revlon and Mary Kay
To hide her guise under demise.
See through and realize
That all deception is…
Is lies.

What is Fear?

Fear is that thing, that monster,
That makes you lock the car doors
When I come by,
Peering through your blinds
Avoiding my eyes.
It was the thing that kept the blacks doing
Chores,
Whipping them while they lay on the floor
On all fours.
Fear was the thing that had blacks lynched
And burned,
Kept out of schools not allowed to learn.
It was fear, I fear, that killed Mr. King,
Kennedy, Angela Davis fled, kept Ali out
The ring.
It was fear that "separated our fingers".
It's fear, I figure,
That accidentally forces cops to pull the
Trigger.
Fear is what makes us content
To live without minority presidents.
Fear is what made whites want to ship us
Back,
Which is kind of the same as introducing
Crack because then we are not your problem
And if we were, you wouldn't solve 'em.
Fear has innocent men in penitentiaries
And unlucky counterparts in cemeteries.
Fear, it is what caused the American
Revolution.
Attucks's death the beginning of a
Resolution.
Fear is what got the best of Emmett Till

And the Scottsboro boys even with the truth
Revealed.
Fear lies about depression, inverse, flip
It around, turn it backwards, it reads
Recession.
Fear is what caught Saddam,
Even though I thought Osama was supposed to
Be the problem—
American planes into the Trade Centers a
Natural bomb.
Fear separates church from state,
Fear that God Blessing America will make it
Ok.
Fear is the homosexual issue left alone
I never knew Steve came from Adam's bone.
Fear is what sent us to Vietnam
And has our soldiers in Iraq for far too
Long.
Fear is resistance to listen.
Close your eyes, plug your ears, and forget
The mission.
Fear wants to eliminate Affirmative Action,
Reducing minorities' power by just a
Fraction.
Fear is what started the Underground
Railroad.
Fear is why some of the slaves told.
Fear is the reason Jesus was slain,
Slapped, scorn, beaten, enduring so much
Pain.
Fear created the glass ceilings,
We can look through and see what Enron's
Revealing.
Fear is what created sin, racism, and hate.

And courage is the only thing that can set
Things straight.

Immortal

When the sun rises with the new day dawning
And exposes pestilence's well hidden face
There will be no space,
There will be no meter,
There will be no time.
Only the silent collapse
(as air leaving the lungs from a sudden
thrust)
Of voice,
The illusion of choice,
And the lurid awareness
That this life is closing.
And in that moment also will exist
One of two resolves:
A calm from the cathartic push of words
Birthed from the depth of the soul,
Nursed by the umbilical thought of the
Brain,
And forged through perfect tongues;
Or
A restlessness, a resolve of bitter
Resentment at the squander of opportunity,
Despise for the resulting demise, and
Hatred at the silent caption marking your
Tomb.
For all great men leave behind a trail of
Letters,

And when they are pieced back together,
Words form, resurrecting their lives as a
Phoenix from the bowels of heart's ashes in
Incantation.
Sleep comes for us all,
But all great men can be conjured to live
Forever...

Black Thought

Black thought stems from what the blacks
Fought for, hymns
"We shall overcome" that sound.
Drowning out the many whip cracks across
The back,
Searching underground for the railroad
Losing track.
The North Star, the aim of the trek and
Mossy patches.
Patches from the quilts we made fashioned
For those who lay in the grave,
Who *paved* the way laying bricks for the
W.P.A.
Hoover, Crow, and Thurmond couldn't have
Their way.
Griots still heard today,
Messages echoing across time and sea.
Across sardined packed ships and mothers'
Spread hips-
For Masters forcing the issue through their
Lips.

Mulattos dragged by trucks through the
Woodchips,
Hanged from trees at all degrees
For looking at white women or drawing the
Wrath of the ghostly sheets by… being.
Grandfathers beginning to buckle,
But God supports their knees,
Supports their needs.
Hughes and Renaissance and Black Panther's
Stalking the grounds,
Guarding the infants of the holy grounds
On top of mounds,
Body piles reaching the sky.
The Wiz, Sammy Davis, and Mr. Hines.
Our heritage is scattered and hard to
Outline.
Cops sprinkling crack on blacks to set them
Back,
And hide their hate for the color of which
We can't escape.
Lucy in the Sky with Diamonds playing on
Tape,
To control our brains and padlock it with a
Platinum chain.
A preventative measure to limit the right
To obtain their true history
And discourage pride.
Killing each other,
Wastin' our ancestors' time,
Carrying the cup to fill their mind,
And pass on the torch to the next in line,
Preexistence of Black thought from a land
Before the land of time.

Test

The paradoxical and toxical ingredients I
Think they put in breast,
To make those double d's bigger and badder
Than the rest.
The same place babes and infants are quick
To rest,
Is often for some men the end of the quest.
They should instead invest,
In a lady's mind clothed in a women's vest.
For everything that is real…
Test.
The Pastors in the pulpit giving
Doxological trues to free the minds of
Congregational groupies-
Clutching rosy rosaries,
Eyes clenched tight praying hard for
Something to touch them ovaries.
Watch it!
Prophets pocketing God's profits while poor
People struggle to make less—
For everything that is real…
Test.
For the man following the
Drum home in his chest.
Fighting to find his way while on all sides
He is pressed.
When it seems like the most logical answer
Is a guess,
For everything that is real…
Test.
Women, soft whispers
In those ears to impress
And move you to undress from that dress.

Lying breast to breast
Under his gentle caress
You feel love,
He feels like getting dressed.
For everything that is real…
Test.
Men, some ladies have
Their noses in the air
Until the bright glimpse
Of that watch's glare.
Unlock that neck, Unlock that smile,
And unlock those legs if your funds you'll
Share—
Before you think you've been blessed,
For everything that is real…
Test.
When all the faith in the world lies with
The faithless and the faithful have lost
All of their hope and zest.
And then you question whose religion is the
Best,
For everything that is real…
Test.

Mirrors

I think the other day I awoke and thought
That the world was comprised of
Reflections,
And patriarchs in conception.
Who despite double-wrapped contraception
Still manage to impregnate and birth
Perception by releasing infection.
(Aahhhhh!!!)
I know it's a lot for a first morning
Thought,
But still...the thought persisted,
Cysted,
Ever since then
No desisting,
A consistent,
Reminiscent reminder
That the world is
Comprised of reflections—
As I journey throughout the day
Before I even form my mouth
To say "Hello"
I peered into the windows of your soul
And felt the power of recognition grow
And grow and grow
And presumably know
Exactly what I was all about
Through the reflection of the deep dark sea
Lying before you.
But what you didn't see, mind you,
Was the reflection of me of you in me.
In my eyes and skin the strength of onyx,
And a reflection of your near black heart,

Of your full black art,
Of corruption and destruction
That reproduces malfunction
At a particular junction.
Whew!!!
I shudder to think
Of these reflections,
And the connections that lie inside of
Those unfirst impressions.
Yes, I think it was the other day that I
Realized,
The world is comprised of reflections.

Trophies

The breeze blows gently
Through the trees as bodies swing
Effortlessly through the air
Because their burden has been dropped,
Burned out, cut out
Poured out onto the ground is life's juice.
And the crowds stand round about
And the smallest devils give jubilation
Held by their mothers' undesirable laps.
And women cook as men record
Their trophies in historical books.
A picnic on a sunny day with
Dark hearts behind veneer smiles.
Many trophies have been captured by man in
This way: deer's head, swordfish, and the
Heart of the Nile.

Boy meets Girl

Boy meets girl,
Girl is amused.
Boy beats girl,
Girl is confused.
Do it again, then enthused.
Do it again, then in love.
Do it again, crush her body,
send her soul above.
Boy meets girl.

The Calling

Distant thumps, thunderous sounds.
Vibrations pulsing from deep in the ground.
Out of the heart of Africa,
That is where real music came.
From the roaring drum and surged through
The sugar cane.
And though far from its origin the drum
Doesn't fade,
But pushes on through monsoonious rain.
It grows in strength as another son or
Daughter awakens and joins in the tune.
Boom!
Boom!
Boom!
Because we have drums for hearts
That beat and resound and
Carry any doubt asunder.

The sound you hear in me is Africa's
Thunder.

Ribs

I am just an admirer of a fine piece of
Art, noticing all of the strokes the artist
Took care to create.
Smooth glides from the brush despite the
Mistakes.
God's outstretched hand spanning time with
Life in the finger.
Creating Adam while still on his lips the
Words linger.
And realizing that it was not good for man
To be alone,
From his sides he took a single bone.
And before Adam could utter a single groan,
God had fashioned a woman from his own.
Who would ever know that the God who takes
And gives could produce sweet,
Precious life from a single rib.

Soulutions

Is it less soulful when we don't soulidify
Soulutions?
Disqualifying people soulely on appearance
Apart from character?
Ignoring the souliloquy
And the cry of an oppressed race,
Watching them soulicit; selling drugs by
The case that somehow was the wrong thing
Left in the right *place*
To be found...
Soulutions.
Found in the soulidarity of the dark place
Being held in low regard as a disgrace
Because of burnt sienna crayola traces.
Proclaimed stupid based on soulecisms
But who is really in the dark silhouettes?
Souligisms exist of the soulphistications
Even though we were denied education at
First,
We have improved access now
And when given the chance there are
Opportunities to astound and abound.
Soulutions: crack, ignorance, poverty, and
Chains for blacks.
Soulutions none the less,
But whose soulution is that?

W.M.D.

Where are the weapons of mass destruction?
Where are the threats that could destroy
The nation?
Try checking the White house
In the presidential station
With the potential to march our country
To hell in haste aaannd—
Minute "Rice" in the boiling pot,
Ben Veniste keeping it hot while trying to
Uncover the plot.
Check in our schools destructive tools.
Revolution evolution taught by fools.
It's a poison,
D-con slipped between the pages
Spoiling the minds of our future sages.
Some say the weapons of mass destruction
Are in our church and...
Priests cornering altar boys
Behind the curtain,
And we can't be certain
If Bush really knew, but
We know that he had a clue and what would
He do if he got clued again?
Weapons of mass destruction like the Klan—
A Christian cause with a Christian plan.
Weapons of mass destruction like school
Shootings,
Somethings amok constantly polluting.
Weapons of mass destruction like 500 yard
Snipers, bullets piercing heads,
The stinging of a million vipers.
Weapons of mass destruction like the
Oppression of the poor,

Laying on our streets
While the rich ask for more.
Weapons of mass destruction like the
Special homosexual.
Weapons of mass destruction like drugs and
Guns killing our nation,
But where do they come from?
"We must find weapons of mass destructions"
Bush stated loud and clear...
But I wonder...
Does he know those weapons of mass
Destruction are here?

El Voz

I have found my voice.
I stretched my cords
and opened wide
and **Screamed**
and still remained only faintly audible—
It will take more,
A score of people just like me,
and you've heard us before.
I know it.
My band of brothers and sisters—called
Poets.

Nine Months of Labor

Hate was probably something that started
Small.
All and all,
Wasn't noticeable at all.
Potential energy of an infectious disease
Spreading, embedding.
Breeding, exceeding
Presenting claims that are often
Misleading.
Hiding…
In a small stowaway in the cubbyhole heart.
It grew and simmered long before people had
Races
And ran races
And ran to escape its anger.
It despised the changing of the status quo
And it resisted our attempts to overthrow
Its reign of terror,
Its rain of terror.
Its colors ran scattered,
Covering the earth from birth
Making hate that much worse.
It practiced, patiently perfecting its art,
A seeping gas sitting, awaiting a spark,
A catalytic start that was a lifetime in
The making,
Leaving jaws gaping and eyes
Sagging from all its nagging.
You can't sleep on Hate.
And the world was unprepared for the burden
Hate had been dragging.
Hate for colors, hate for races,

Hate for people from opposite places, hate
For positions,
Hate for decisions.
Hate for those who spoke and hate for those
Who listened.
The disease inflicted everyone
And everyone drank from its intoxicating
Goblet.
Some even hated themselves…yes,
This was how hate excelled.
Using Genocidic means to extinguish nations
Jews, Africans, Arabs, and Asians.
Who next you ask?
The world,
Until it's a memory of a distant past.
And what now, you ask of the xenophobe?
Hate still dwells and lurks awaiting its
Chance.
Shake speared the subject through with a
Lance
When he discussed how it affected Romeo and
Juliet's romance.
There may be a way, perchance,
For you to avoid Medusa's glance.
But be sure of this one thing,
Hate won't sleep until the whole world
Joins its dance.

Alcoholics Anonymous

If I were an alcoholic
The A.A. would genuinely work to appease
The monster I created, my personal disease.
But grudgingly another A.A. works for these,
Giving rights and equity to those victims
Of means seized not only by small poxian Schemes,
But the racist prison
Spanning the seas.
The Intoxicating disease that drunkingly
Pleases those who hate the things that God Creates.
That's why I check the box asking my model
And make in a system where they have to
Force themselves to love, but they can't Relate.
Though they have the "smarter brains"
They just can't seem to comprehend why we hate those binding chains.
"Just move on and be as separate as fingers."
The effects of those words still linger
In my ears' catacomb.
Invisible lines of separate but equal,
Separate systems; integration for some
Proved to be lethal.
And I am quite sure that the abolition of A.A.
Would manufacture, no doubt, a sequel.
Many minorities just couldn't bear it
When told, why not be evaluated based on Merit?

They knew better…
So, I'll take what they give me and more,
Slowly until power is relinquished to the
Hands of the poor.
They may hold the keys,
But I am building a door.
So that all may pass and that's an
Affirmative action.

Types of Stereos

Maybe it all started with the smell,
The pungent smell of seared flesh burning
Branded, tarred and feathered.
Maybe the love for chicken developed as
Such…
Maybe it all started as a
A memorial.
Euphoreal feelings for watermelon,
Spittin' seeds, digging holes for graves,
Plantin' seeds.
Was it truly so wrong to conceive the idea
Of being free?
Maybe we run so fast because we are so far
Behind,
Or we talk loud because it is so hard to be
Heard.
Maybe my dick is so big to carry the load,
While praying to the one who holds all.
Maybe my lips are big because I have so
Much to say.
Maybe my nose is so wide to inhale life,

Taking deep breaths while the system
Smothers my light.
Maybe I dance so well from dodging death,
All the while questioning if it were the
Best option left.
Maybe we entertain to be noticed,
Be a person, not just a quota.
Or maybe we entertain to please,
To overcome the "invisible" disease.
Maybe I smoke weed to escape
The sight of bodies murdered through the
Night,
Of my brethren, by my brethren and mankind,
Out of sight, out of mind, inviting my
Plight.
Maybe I love music because it touches my
Soul,
And I turn it up loud to drown out the pain
From the blows.
Maybe I am so angry "for no reason" at
Being kidnapped,
Suppressed,
And disconnected from my tree root for
several seasons.
It took a movement for improvement.
Maybe even *your* eyes that can see so clear,
Can't see the flies on the plantation from
The stench of death near.
Whatever the reason, it's clear to see
That maybe I'm not the maybe you thought of
Me…

Pardon Me

Don't be offended by my hate for the
Confederate flag,
Or the anger that rushes my veins when I
Hear that they dragged
The river looking
For a body to deliver to families
Quivering, awaiting the news.
I get offended when they say that the
Problem of the past is the past's problem.
And that the problem with blacks is that
They won't get off their asses—
That we seek the path of unsuccess.
Don't be offended by my lack of respect for
The law,
Smothering the mouse under its paw.
I get offended when I get stopped by the
Cops,
Asked to get out of my car while others
Watch.
I get offended when I am your example of
Exertion of power so don't get offended
When I tell you the hour
Has come for restitution...
New heart, new soul, new mind...revolution

Souletry

It all began with the people.
It began with the rich oral tradition of
Seeing,
Retaining, and then speaking to the
Children,
The precious pearls of our oysters.
Those pearls took that tradition and added
Flava to *savor*, *marinata* in your mind.
As they struggled to make the uphill climb,
Rewinding to a time when some gave their
Lives for the cause which varied for
Cultures,
But all sought to disrupt status quo laws.
Now I have the privilege to speak with my
Experience and a foreknowledge that
Connects me to my heritage and asks,
"Are you here for the cause or because?"
I wasn't there in the beginning,
But I contribute to the task.
I hear it through the music and catch
Glimpses when I read.
Its deep seeded roots lie smack center,
Slightly left of aorta and north from
ventricle.
That is how I know.
When it came from the drum, from the beat
And the feet of the people it was POETRY.
When it flowed down from the mountain to my
Mind it was FLOETRY.
Now it pours from my heart and leaks from
My soul to the streets…Now it is SOULETRY!

The Love Letter

I...
I feel your hand caressing my body,
Taking so much care.
The warmth of your touch reminds me how
You love me so much.
And I know you're enchanted by my glare
The sleekness I wear and the way I produce
Humility and meekness with my stare.
You push all of my buttons,
I feed on you eternally glutton.
Gently you take my shaft in your hand,
We are in the love jones
And your wish is my command.
Our intense love heightens
And my only concern is for you to...
To arrive and so I drive,
And I feel your grip tighten gently around
My shaft—
Fully and totally entranced by your craft—
You give me a quick hard jerk with your
Hand and now I understand.
My job, my desire is to help you arrive.
First me and then you.
You receive me into your mouth stretch,
Stretched, stretching it out.
I feel your tongue searching it out.
I feel the pressure from your squeeze
And I can't fight anymore, I release,
Ahhhh!!!
Then I relax with ease.
Perfect timing we go at the same time
And I can't help but think that somewhere
Lodged deep in your mind is a piece of me.

You see some call the love we shared a
Disease.
Spread by the pressures of life,
Intellectual ingratitude expressed by his
Attitude,
At the school miseducation by fools,
The tools which successfully unequip
Students for the duel.
You see some call the love we shared a
Disease.
Harassed by cops, still unharvested crops.
Waiting to be reaped by a farmer other than
The reaper—
The creeper—
It's cheaper to cheapen life with the suds
From the Heineken and to take a hit of the
"I Believe I Can Fly" again than to face
the Cries again,
As a crouched mother embraces a son dying
In the street.
You see some call the love we shared a
Disease,
But I remind you that I put your mind at
Ease.
Children, lame, crippled
By the absence of a man
With a well thought out plan.
I can, my love understand,
Why I am in such demand.
When the times got rough you were there
And I was the one.
And now that I arrived and so did you
I guess our times together are done.
I will love you always and forever, your
friend, your love.   −Gun

History began with America

History began with America.
Didn't you know?
Not Iroquois, Sioux, or Nava-who?
Oh, but in 1492 Christopher Columbus
Sailed the …
But didn't have a clue.
Stir the stew and view
What the melting pot can do, marinatin'
And creating Cablanasian brews.
History began with America,
Didn't you know?
That America evolved from Plymouth Rocks
Spooks invading with small cocks and small
Pox.
The voices of apparitions walk and talk.
Giving witness to the predators stalking,
Stinging,
Ringing, bringing the "black plague"
With them in boats, souls and eyes
Lifted keeping the boats afloat—hands
Interlocked.
Praying, shocked? Don't be.
History began with America.
Didn't you know?
Bring us your tired, poor, your huddled
Masses.
And have them pledge allegiance to the
America rag evolved from Confederacy tags,
Forced trues,
Forced gags—these are things we fail to
Find in history books.

The same things that shook and hooked our
Nation rocked is our foundation.
And so we hide and lock our pride
Behind our silence.
Ask questions, learn lessons, mature your
Knowledge to adult from adolescence.
What could cause pure hate to arbor and
Force Japan upon Pearl Harbor, was it
Power?
What was gained by knocking down towers,
For what and for whom?
As chalked buildings and dust swarm
Smell the fumes and become aware indeed of
What is happening?
America was built on the poor man's dream
And it took a team of savvy, highly
Qualified niggers,
Spics, and red-faced savages, chinks,
Gooks, towel headed freaks to make ends
Meet,
Who still strive to erect this country.
History began with America.
Didn't you know?
You change history upon entering the scene—
You are no longer just African, Asian,
And lets get even more, creative, a Native.
But you apply for the surname of shame
It's strange to join forces with the
Sources of your pain.
American—everything that has ever been
Right,
They write and we read and absorb and
Everything that has ever been wrong is lost
In a forgotten song,
But stay strong.

Delve deeper into the darkened dwellings
Research and study and you'll discover some
Things you never knew and hopefully grow
One way or the other—
History began with America, didn't you
Know?
Discover and uncover that slavery did exist
And how many slaves braved the risk to
Escape.
Or you might need a push to understand that
Prescott Bush a.k.a. the "shitler" was the
Same man who funded Hitler
And now we live in this Saddam and Gomorrah
Where we believe the lies that we are
Liberating.
The horrors and atrocities and the gore,
But we can't free the whores from poverty
Or rid the disease infesting our streets—
Books don't tell this,
All you receive are the pretty posies
To the point where shit is real good
Smelling
And swelling your head—
Don't believe the lies,
Because if History began with America,
You and me would be dead.

A Brief Review

I fully and militantly embrace,
The color, the absence, the culture, the
Race,
The blackness I dwell in—
Inhale, exhale the brief history.
Still surrendering my soul to the black
Hole,
The abyss of dark Hughes, please excuse me
If I wander down the stream reading books
By Brooks.
My soul is carried to the streets;
The fight for rights in the Ali where I
Meet face to face with the nemesis, the
Antithesis.
The one who moved us from the village in
Africa to the shack in the field to project
Hood.
I should begin at the beginning where the
War first raged and was waged.
Where the Ashanti, the Mandingo, and the
Zulu (and many others) payed with slaves to
Protect themselves from the slave trade
With weapons.
Progressin' stepping over the bodies while
They lay suffocating from the fumes of
Defecation.
Some like Cinque calling out to God
With weapons shod
Overthrowing ships like the Amistad.
Facing the prods standing in line being
Poked with rods an exchange of gods from
The Pharoahs in Egypt
To those who seized it.

Checking the size, opening mouths,
Giving muscles a feel.
Who belongs in the kitchen?
Who belongs in the field?
What do the consequences yield?
And thus began the plot to escape
Where the brave and resourceful found paths
Leading to freedom underground.
Now don't get me wrong,
There were happy times and at the end of
The year there were parties as I rewind to
Douglass's time.
But it was to bribe the slaves
And condone the acts.
After a drought, God brought us out.
Lincoln sought to take slavery from the
South weakening the opponent for the next
Bout.
Of course, this period had many prophets,
Ushering, guiding, seeking,
Providing the way.
It had many Sojourners for truth,
Strong willed,
Skilled with no fear of fear which birthed
Many engineers in the weeds of abductors.
Which also happened to produce many
Conductors who surged resisting the urge to
Drown themselves in the tub.
Man!
Freedom is visible leavin' our captors to
Feel Garrisoned and trapped.
Shortly after the South began to collapse
And after some time elapsed,
Africans discovered they were free.
Or so they thought they would be,

But in actuality they switched
Penitentiaries.
Bad omens when vultures circle the sky.
Holidays became a time for strange fruit.
Long before David Duke's era,
The Klan was forcing terror
And knocking us down and down
Forcing our faces to the ground
Until we were grounded.
Astounded, surrounded
On all sides and still we would rise
To our opponents surprise,
Confounding our opponents
By our positive demise.
We combined and converted our
Lyrical hope to spiritual
As the ethereal hope of our cries
Rise to the ears of a deaf sky.
Mistletoes and blows while Bo's jingles
Flow.
It shows and time only tells
The future's hand
And the grounds demanding
The new coming of age
The presence of a new sage,
One to pass on the knowledge of the
Cullen's, Carmichael's, Davis's, and
Pratt's, and Dyson's
And feed the hungry mouth's of our youths,
The same ones filled with the chipped *teeth*
From swallowing the same cold hard truths.

The Headless Horseman

Charging, galloping, the marauder
Marauding.
Saving the damned damsel in distress,
the audience applauding.
It's the headless horseman
Causing the ooohing and aaahing.
His headlessness prevents cap from
Shodding,
Donning,
Dawning sun peeks out just above the
Awning,
Yawning after a good night's rest following
The night's frolicking heroics of scaling
Scaled dragons laying lair.
Penetrating impenetrable layer of armor
With diamond tipped blade,
Pillages of villages,
Fields on fire burning.
Children and women scurrying
As tales of the horsemen
Scatter to and fro in rumors illuminated in
The tales of white haired bearded crinkles.
Shadows dancing off of hidden cavern walls
As the halls of children's mouths crack and
Gape, eluding tales of the horsemen escape
In tavern tradition of *his* large long
Fingers wrapped around the nape of one
Helpless in his grasp.
Even more eluding is the tale of the head
Lost at the hands of some ambitious youth
On quest,
Testing his brawn and wit against rumors
Cast of the evil Lochness lurking,

Creeping, curling, hurling him through the
Wretched depths.
And the heroic last effort as the bittered
Teen in lost archetypal fashion,
Cocks his broken blade,
Snapped slightly above the hilt,
And forcing it forward,
Lets the last moment's guilt drip.
Then limping his way to triumph knowing it
Was evil's sinful blood he spilt when he
Split the darkened vessel,
He reaches the villager's lost souls and
It's the head he hoists in the air with a
taunt.
But circumventing at ancient battle ground
Is the unrest of one headless soul's haunt
And new gauntless figures kneel
In dust kicked trails as saddles blaze and
Instead of innocent bodies,
He whisks victim's souls to the grave—
Until another youthful spirit,
Braver than the last,
Vanquishes the wraith's rage or a brainless
Knave returns the skull of the headless
Horsemen to his grave.

N.I.G.G.A.S. from Another Planet

<u>N</u>ever <u>i</u>ndigenous <u>g</u>enerations <u>g</u>enerating
<u>a</u>daptations for <u>s</u>urvival,
n.i.g.g.a.s.
Destined to be displaced despite their
discontentment until they make that mecca—
revival.
No Cinderella slippers to slip onto those
slipping,
In that life fluid dripping, dropping--
life energy dipping,
life's fist losing the gripping—
Why?
We're niggas from another planet and though
few cannibals understand it,
They were the ones who demanded it,
manufactured and canned it—
"free labor in a can" Sloooowwwgaaan
Sloowww gain—slow pain searing the flesh,
branded "N's" keloid on their chest, never
slowing, no rest.
<u>N</u>ew <u>i</u>ntellectual <u>g</u>atherings <u>g</u>lowing from
their <u>a</u>spiring <u>s</u>ong,
n.i.g.g.a.s.
Niggas in the field singing to survive the
long day.
<u>N</u>ow <u>i</u>nstigating <u>g</u>rimy <u>g</u>luttons <u>a</u>sk for
<u>s</u>hips,
n.i.g.g.a.s.
For a means to whisk us away to uproot an
oak or a sycamore to sick 'em more
made some sick and others more dead,
heads rollin' to avoid taste and
mastication.

Natives **i**nsecure about **g**rouping with
gorilla **A**merican **s**hit,
n.i.g.g.a.s.,
and the diseases that pit
one life against the gun.
Or how 'bout the life of a son too young to
know "the man" is the one who will only
view him as **n**ew **i**ntimidation **g**urgling since
geography **a**ssimilated this **s**in,
n.i.g.g.a.s.
As he stares down the barrel of the gun
it's a nigga that shows through the scope
across the scope of land and my son's **n**ew
intelligence,**g**rowing **g**enerosity, and
apparent **s**incerity makin'
n.i.g.g.a.s.
Too young to understand that he's a nigga
in they eyes,
that's how he'll be seen behind tactile
eyes—
those eyes that feel you before your mouth
spreads wide.
Now **I** **g**ive **g**lory for my **a**spiring **s**oul,
n.i.g.g.a.s.,
because eventually I'll have to pay the
toll either to interstate 666 or Rt. 777.
Sometimes a person's hate outweighs their
desire to go to heaven or maybe my heaven
is the same as some,
a **n**orth **i**ntervention past **g**hosts and
goblins and **a**ssassinated **s**aints,
n.i.g.g.a.s.
Can't wasn't vernacular to those who
succeeded—

By any means necessary as little Malcolm
would teach it, preach it and the south's
attempts to succeed it,
until fate forced them to concede it.
But forget the past, we're in a new age and
cage.
And we ignored all the signs felt along the
way until K-K-Kramer reminded us one day
that "He's a nigger, He's a nigger, and
He's a nigger" he pulled the trigger;
because we were never supposed to figure—
it was a man's best secret, that if I
didn't know my neighbor's feelings, that's
how he would keep it.
I mean **n**iggas **i**gnorance in a **g**lossy **g**lass
will **a**lways keeps us **s**eparate,
n.i.g.g.a.s.
But I guess at last the world finally grew
and realized that if your **n**ative **i**ntellect
gives the **g**ears **a** final **s**pin,
n.i.g.g.a.s. ,
the spin is true.
If you're calling me a nigga you're
probably a nigga too!
I and the people like me don't belong here,
but were damned and at the same time
demanding:
I'm a nigga from another planet—ship my ass
back to where it first landed….

The Sound of Music

Bee do boo- Bee do boo- Bee do boo
Rhythms spastic static spanning elastic the
Stretch of time.
Bee do boo-Bee do boo- Bee do boo
Sonic sweet sultry suite songs 'splayed
Line by line.
Bee do boo-Bee do boo-Bee do boo
Sounds synthesized into syndication.
Bee do boo- Bee do bop
Masterfully mimicking monotonous monologue
Meeting of the mimes; meeting of the minds
Through the mastication of mine.
Bee do boo-Bee do boo bop
Sassy sexy saxy tunes bait us.
Bee do boo- Bee do boo
Tall trumpet sounds lift us by Davis,
Glittery Glossy conglomerate glows
From Satchmo.
Whistling whittles weeping willow
Daughters.
Bee do boo
Sirens rising from the cold murky grave of
Muddy Waters.
Catching cohesive collisions
From complicated Coltrane.
Smooth, fluid movements
Just arranged
With no brain
Playing heart strings…

Two Women in the Street Crying

Bent knees against the gravel scraping,
Stomach burning,
Eyes stinging,
Shots echoing,
Screams ringing.
"Signs of the times"
That's what her Pastor will say.
In her lap lays the head of her child
His trigger hand twitching than residing at rest.
Two wrinkled hands clutched to hold the pain in her chest.
No audible sound from open mouth in unrest.
In a murky puddle, her reflection can be seen
somewhere, uptown, suburbs, no boarded houses between,
shiny, clean, military car
formal telegram from afar.
Bent knees carpet burned.
Stomach churned.
Lesson learned.
As they place the son in the urn.
Turning to carefully place the urn on the table,
next to the folded flag.
The Private swivels catching the mother who
Begins to stagger.
Two women in the street crying.
Two sons lost to bullets flying.
I can't for the life in me stop trying
to understand
Why life from death's hands keeps prying?

A young girl selling her body
to pay the toll of life.
Her mother questions,
"What happened to the baby I used to know?"
Demons eating away her flesh to expose her soul.
"Tis the sign of the times"
That's what her priest will say.
Halfway around the world
not too far away.
A young boy searches for diamonds in a cave
As militant guerillas scream orders over
distant shots fired.
The boy returns empty handed
So home he returns "empty handed".
Stumps dripping blood dried,
Two clear paths running trails down a dirty face.
Two women in the street crying,
for a childhood killed before its time
I can't for the life in me stop trying
to understand why life at death's table
continues to dine.

Cycle

Violence produces violence,
Sense,
some tried peace,
hence,
Piece by piece
Cease.
Poor before broken edges sharp guard
Fast throats gagged slow
As life closes.
Why?
Closes life as
Slow gagged throats fast.
Sharp edges broken,
Before shards reconstructed poor.
Cease,
Piece by piece.
Hence peace tried some, *since*
Violence produces violence.
Why?

Big Brother

Always watching,
Stalking,
Talking...
Mom says to love Big Brother
in all of his hate.
Encouraging me this phase will pass,
just wait.
The weight overloading, hard enduring
grab your pockets, contents securing

as Big Brother ankle hoisting, shaking
　　　　　Voice quivering as I scream,
　　　　　　　stomach churning.
　　　　　　Tripping on my journey,
　　　　　　Face in mud sticking,
　　　　　Big Brother hair pulling,
　　He's not bullying, he's Big Brothering.
　　　　Hovering, covering, smothering
　Common sense teaches you to hide your cents
　　since sixth sense taught Big Brother to
　　　　　　snatch your cents.
　　　　"No…not Big Brother" dad says
　　He's a Patriot acting in best interest.
　　I'll take care to warn my children of Big
　　　　　　　　brother
　　　"Kids, watch out for your Uncle Sam.
　　　　　　　He's a bitch!"

Family Tree

He wakes up in the morning and kisses his Spouse;
He wakes up in the morning and kisses his Girl.
He goes to the river sees his reflection
And vomits;
He goes to the sink see his reflection and
Vomits.
He knows today is the day at hand.
He grabs his war paint, begins his mask;
He ties his color rags takes a hit from a
Silver flask.
He sharpens his feathered iron spear to
Prepare for battle;

He loads his gun ready for war.
He hugs his son as he leaves the hut;
He kisses his son screwing from the pain in
His gut.
He sets out on foot to stalk the woods;
He hops in the "caddy" uses the wood.
He creeps low amongst the shadows;
He drives slow bass banging sticattos.
He sees his enemy.
He locks in on his target.
He pills' the vill';
He shoots to kill.
He takes what he can.
He takes what he can.
Becoming a man,
He returns to his hut;
He returns to his 'hood.
Spoils to the victor.
Similarities seem to be.
Part of the Family Tree.

Just a thought...

My grandfather's shoulders used to shake.
They would tremble and quake in the wake of
His booming voice.
His voice would echo down hall's corridors
Sometimes the walls would shake,
But I was not scared.
My shoulders would shake too
And sometimes one clear blue tear
Would form in my eye's corner before
Dropping
Far, far below.

My head would take shelter in my elbow's
Nook.
But I was not sad.
As I watched my grandfather, my knees would
Sometimes buckle,
And I would have to seat myself to keep
From losing my balance.
But I was not ill.
I would slam my fist down on the table.
I would kick my legs into the air
And knock things onto the floor.
My voice would raise in high pitched
Squeals.
But I was not angry.
Yet I still remember it like yesterday,
The joke he told.

Grow up

I don't have to wear my pants below my
Waist
To know my efforts are wasted if it's a
Woman I chase.
And it doesn't take a pro to know,
It's not all about the gems
Or about how many spokes are on your rims.
A realist might even realize the slim
Splinter of being an
Athletic star,

With enough money to have more than two or
Three cars.
And understand that the only place I might
Rap is on some corner with some old cat.
But the fact of the matter remains
That you shouldn't live to gain,
But that you should gain through living.
And if somewhere in that tandem
You should stumble across
A golden ticket in a drain,
Or a distant uncle's remains,
Or at cash register receive some
Very, very rare change in an exchange.
Then the veins of this life are enriched
But not richer in vain.

A Note

A simple note
To say "hi"
To say "goodbye"
And to sum farewell,
As the sleek dragon
With no tongue
And no scales
Only fire breathing
Double nostrils',
Hot breath on my neck
Until it sucks in one more final heave
And
      L   W
B   O   S!

To You

To You...
I am the stain on existence.
The scuff mark remnant of a shoe's soul.
I am the blemished lamb;
The facial birthmark on America.
I am proof of a story rarely told.
I am...
The worm in your apple—
I am the pebble in your shoe,
The scar remaining.
I am the question mark with an asterisk.
I am the painful scab, a black lung, the
Last rung.
I am my father's, father's, father hanged.
I am a migraine,
I am...
A blackout over a city.
I am blacklisted,
A bad apple not far from the tree.
I am rude and inaudibly loud.
I am winter's solitude,
Your clouded vision.
I am a rotten stench in your nasal cavity.
I am an aftertaste,
A passing thought.
I am a wallflower, the blacksheep of my
American family.
I am the idiot savant.
I am the gap, the dark side.
I am a burden and a privilege.
I am a fading memory and a reminder.

I am Cain and Abel to stand tall, proud,
And strong.
To you
I am this song.

A Strange Niceness

It was hidden behind a smile,
The fact that I didn't belong.
And the calculated suggestion was so
carefully, gently, intelligently placed;
That my fit may be more "Cinderella-like"
elsewhere.
It was implied
That the glass slipper shipped to my
doorstep was a Crisco fit,
And that I might better enjoy a Nike
Or the shoe with the little cat on it
That no one would think I'd know;
(it's a Puma)
Nah.Nah.
To the rest of the world
It was a "set-up" date.
A favor.
It was a practiced kiss.
Pity sex.
Leaving my dignity under the covers,
As she turns and walks out the door
Never looking back
Or saying
Goodbye.

The Breath

The funk, the stench, the breath.
The height of peace is death.
The floor of knowledge is depth.
Hope is when nothing is left,
and still,
Somehow you hold.
Waiting for coal to turn gold.
A dream is always half real,
kept alive by desire's appeal.
And effort can't always be measured by
yield.
So one waits for dreams to congeal
and when like a scab it heals
and flesh's weaknesses are again concealed.
And the scar that still remains
Shows the growth of self over pain.
And when the scar-covered corpse is all
that's left.
It's void of the funk,
The stench,
The breath.

A Day in the Life of Steve Green

I woke up to brown this morning.
Smooth brown skin,
soft, brown eyes
old, brown banana peels with black patches
in front of my college dorm hallway.
Gorillas.
And the gorilla in me can't understand
why despite numerous postings to "Do Not
Feed the Animals",
they continue to feed the beast.
Failing to realize that once the beast has
had its fill
from their maggot infested meal,
with its swollen stomach ready to split
at the seams from the hurt concealed.
The anguish unleashed won't leave room to
hide behind missing bed linens.
You won't be able to stand behind a
whispered "Nigger".
You will not be able to shield yourself
from my wrath.
The only cleansing bath will be in the
remains of the aftermath from my spewing.

Ode to a Patriarch

To a man who taught me
What it means to be a Patriarch.
To start the whole thing
From the beginning.
To show his children,
His
Children's children the land of milk and
Honey-
A man who was the definition of fortitude-
To a man, the epitome of progress
Time could not consume
His glorious blooms.
So he triumphed on,
Set to lead his children out of social
Destruction, racial dysfunction,
Recognizing his unction.
He carried us on his back to the land of
Canaan,
The Holy Land, right to the edge.
We overlooked its brim,
Down into all the world had to offer and
With a gentle hand on the small of our back
He ushered us in and remained behind.
On that stormy night when Yahweh saw fit to
Take the Patriarch,
We awoke to continue the legacy and follow
In the steps of the Father and lead our
Children into the Holy Land as well.
Closer to Home, and the Maker, and the
Patriarch.
His song trickled down now for us to bear
The load, where the legacy flows from
Patriarch to ink tipped odes.

To the Eastside

Black people move away from Black people
to get next to white people
who want to get away from Black people.
We can't be equal-
Two separate minds can be found in blacks-
the one who wants to move forward
and the one who can't help but regress.
One takes knowledge to digest
and the other knowledge of the situation
depresses.
Because he realizes the upward climb he
must face,
discouraged by the vertical move of the
race,
plagued by hurdles such as drugs,
dirty, power, hungry cops,
inadequate schools, and economic crisis.
While others take escalators and
elevators-
some remain lost in vices.
I learned African Americans don't not want
success.
That's absurd,
but I heard discouraged is the word.
Progress can be made if fuel is added to
the fire,
if the institutions designed to hinder can
be manipulated to take us higher-
Then and only then we might be able to
enjoy equity over equality
so everyone can obtain their desires.

My Stubborn Mother

With pasty hands
Inside of rubber gloves
And a steaming bucket
Fogging bathroom mirrors,
In a bathroom rich with
The stringent small of
Pine Sol and sweat.
Teaching her young son
How to scrub feverishly around the toilet
And remove the ring from inside of the tub
And clean the deep dark stain
From the grout—
My stubborn mother,
Who refused one sweltering
Summer day to change clothes
In her assigned bathroom.
The one with the putrid smells,
With the piss and the shit
And a dim flickering light faintly
Illuminating the cold, dank, morgue
In that God forsaken hole.
My stubborn mother,
Who made my beautiful Grandmother recommend
To my wise Grandfather that
"We should probably leave before Marshell
Gets us killed"
My stubborn mother,
Who vowed to never again
Be in such a room—
Leaned back against the bathroom door
With both hands on her hips

And watched her son perform
The purifying ritual
Before dashing outside to play.

Grass

They call it the Super-seed
The St. Mary of Jane of Eyre
The funkywilkerbean-
Showing you things you ain't never seen
Producer of clarity.
Relaxer of souls
Stopper of time,
A naked man's clothes.
Weed.
Giving the weak the strength to succeed...
Or Suck seed
How big is weed, when it only takes a
Mustard seed?

A Tribute to M.L.K. Jr.

Thank God
The bullet unleashed
With a crack
Sent to drown
The voice of reason,
The message in the wilderness.
The bullet which
Shattered jaws
And
Exposed spinal cords
Could not silence
The whispers
Of a man who was color blinded
With the vision of a promised land.
Thank God for sending us a King, a leader,
Our Moses.
And may we not forget history.
May we not forget the heaven sent blessing
of our deliverance
from Egypt.

What is Black?

Is it the color of my skin?
The dark, dark hues that keep me out not in?
Is it my mind?
Black thought collective memories of time- my His-tory.
Is it evil that lies within,
warm as a bon fire and ugly as sin?
Is it the moment when I turn out the lights?
Is it just a nigga passin' by?
What is it? You tell me.
Is it something that my eyes cannot see?
Is it something that only I can feel?
Is it my designated town?
Is it my designated seat?
Is it a place where dusty paths never meet feet?
Is it heaven, is it hell?
Is it solitude in jail?
Is it a hole perfectly deep?
Is it a magnet pushing us to opposite sides of the street?
Is it a lever that pushes down the lock?
Is it the hours I put in the clock?
Is it a walk, a talk, or a smell?
Was it the moment when Lucifer fell?
Maybe my definition has failed, so I request the truth.
Is it the blues?
Is it the end of a bruise?

Mother Earth left us no clues.
So I guess the definition of Black "lies"
in You.

About the Author:
Chaz Freeman was born in 1982 in Youngstown, Ohio. He graduated from Cardinal Mooney High School in Youngstown, Ohio and Geneva College in Beaver Falls, Pennsylvania. Currently, he teaches English to middle school students in Central New Jersey. He spends much of his time writing and reading.

www.ingramcontent.com/pod-product-compliance
Lightning Source LLC
Chambersburg PA
CBHW031657040426
42453CB00006B/328